CLEVELAND IS A WARM, FUZZY PLACE

a child's storybook guide to Cleveland

by
Dave Cockley

Photography: Edward T. Neal

CORINTHIANPRESS
Publishing Division of EDR Corporation
3592 Lee Road, Shaker Heights, Ohio 44120 • 216/751-7300

Once upon an afternoon, in an enchanting place called Cleveland, Ohio, there lived a fuzzy, snuggly bear. And his name was Benjamin.

Benjamin was a very bored bear. Can you imagine how boring it is just sitting around waiting to be bear-hugged? Benjamin was also a very curious, adventuresome bear. You could always tell when he was feeling especially curious and adventuresome because his nose would start to twitch.

He lived on a big bed, in a big room, inside a big house. And on this particular day, he had a big, lonesome feeling inside because Missy, the little girl he belonged to, was missing.

Benjamin couldn't find Missy anywhere. As a result, a "cold, prickly" feeling was kicking around inside of Benjamin. And he wanted to have a "warm, fuzzy" feeling. Besides, his nose was twitching.

So Benjamin decided to set out in search of Missy.

Benjamin found a few left-over birthday party balloons bouncing around Missy's bedroom ceiling. He held onto the strings as tightly as he could, opened the window, and away he flew.

Benjamin quickly discovered that flying is fun. He imagined that perhaps people might think he was a "bear-bird". And indeed, he was the fattest, fuzziest "bird" you've ever seen.

Benjamin did attract a few amazed gazes from people below. Mrs. Rumpleplum, who was walking her cat, craned her neck skyward, trying to follow Benjamin's rather haphazard flight. As the wind blew Benjamin and his balloons about, Mrs. Rumpleplum spun around below, trying to watch. Finally, she became so dizzy that she stumbled into Mr. Liverminch's pond —and spent the rest of the day fishing goldfish out of the ruffles in her dress.

Benjamin floated over pretty places to live. Then he floated over big, tall buildings where big people go to work to earn money so they can live in the pretty places. And everything down below looked so-o-o-o small. Benjamin began to wonder if he had grown much bigger or if everything else had grown much smaller.

Benjamin was also wondering how he was going to get back down to the ground to find Missy when he heard a very loud "pop" sound overhead. Then he heard another "pop", then another and another. Benjamin no longer had to worry about how he was going to get down because KER-PLOP, he was down.

Now if it had been you or me, we probably would have broken one of our very brittle bones. But because Benjamin was a fuzzy, snuggly bear, he just bounced a bit. And he said "Ouch!" because he had heard people say "Ouch!" when they fell down.

At first, Benjamin thought he was in a jungle. In fact, he was at the Cleveland Zoo. Missy often came to the zoo with her mommy and daddy, so Benjamin thought he might find her here. He waddled about looking for Missy, watching the animals as he went. And they watched him back with even more curiosity than he watched them.

Guess which zoo animals were Benjamin's favorites?

You're right. He liked the bears best.

Benjamin sat and stared at the bears in their grottos. The Cleveland Zoo is one of the largest and oldest in the country and one of the first to put the lions and tigers and bears and things into natural, open grottos instead of behind bars.

The bears were more interested in finding peanuts that Benjamin and the children threw to them than in finding Missy. But Benjamin was feeling curious and adventuresome again. And his nose began to twitch. So he decided to climb a tree to see if he could spot Missy.

As he started to climb, he thought to himself that it was an awfully fuzzy tree. But it wasn't until he reached the top and discovered two small horns that he realized what he had climbed wasn't a tree at all.

It was a giraffe.

Benjamin was quite surprised to find out that his "tree" was really Wilt, a young giraffe. And Wilt was even more surprised to find a small stuffed bear riding on his neck. He was so surprised that he leaped right out of his grotto and galloped down the highway, causing a very surprised traffic policeman to swallow his whistle.

People poked their heads out of their cars to look way up at Wilt. And Wilt leaned way down to poke his head into cars and look at the people. One cute little car had an artificial flower on the top of its radio antenna, and Wilt leaned over and ate it for lunch.

The long-legged traffic-stopper and his furry, little jockey galloped all the way to Cleveland Hopkins Airport, where several zookeepers finally caught Wilt and took him back to the zoo. Relieved to be safely back on the ground once again, Benjamin daydreamed about being in an airplane flying in the sky where he might be able to peer out and see Missy—when suddenly he found himself flying in the sky.

But he wasn't on a plane. He was flying by the end of his ear, which was being held very tightly by a large hand. At the end of the large hand was a long arm. And at the end of the long arm was a large man in a uniform. And he was chuckling.

The man in the uniform placed Benjamin in the "Lost and Found" at Cleveland Hopkins, which is one of the busiest airports in America. Benjamin knew he would never find Missy as long as he was lost in the "Lost and Found". So he escaped and hopped aboard something called a rapid.

The Cleveland Rapid Transit is one of the few in the United States that go directly from the airport to downtown. Benjamin was moving rapidly toward downtown Cleveland when his nose began to twitch. He decided to climb up on top of the rapid to see if he could see Missy.

Benjamin would have made it had the rapid not jerked around a sharp turn just as he reached the roof. Poor Benjamin flew off the rapid, bounced off a bridge, rolled down a hill—he was very roly-poly—and landed in the middle of a fireworks display.

Or he thought it was fireworks. Actually, Benjamin was staring into a blast furnace that turns iron ore into steel. Cleveland is famous for making the steel that's used to make cars and boats and buildings. And Cleveland makes more machines, more car parts and more paint than any other city in the country.

As he left the steel mill, Benjamin walked along the Cuyahoga River, which flows into Lake Erie. A freighter was steaming up the Cuyahoga, carrying iron ore to the steel mill. Benjamin looked at the huge ship. He looked up and up and up—and up some more. It was the biggest boat he had ever seen.

Then he stumbled over some railroad tracks toward what looked like an enormous bowl of porridge. But when he got to the big bowl, it wasn't a bowl at all. It was Cleveland Municipal Stadium, home of the Indians baseball team and the Browns football team. And instead of porridge, it was filled with people.

Cleveland is one of the few cities with teams in most major sports, including the Cavaliers in basketball, the Indians in baseball, and the Force in indoor soccer.

On this particular afternoon, the big, green field was covered with Cleveland Browns, the most consistently successful team in pro football history. The Browns' kicker was preparing to kick what everyone hoped would be the winning field goal. Just at that moment, Benjamin saw a cute, little golden-haired girl sitting on the other side of the field. "That's Missy!", he thought excitedly to himself.

As Benjamin ran across the field toward a little girl who looked like Missy, he ran in front of the football. In fact, he reached the football at the very same instant that the kicker's foot did. And instead of kicking the ball, KA-POW, the Browns' kicker kicked Benjamin. Benjamin sailed up through the goalposts, winning the game for the Browns and turning 86,000 Browns fans into bear fans, too.

Meanwhile, Benjamin continued to sail over the cheering people, out of the stadium, across the parking lot and, KER-SPLASH, into Lake Erie. Benjamin thought how nice it was for Cleveland to have a lake, where big boats could bring things from around the world and small boats could take people for relaxing rides on weekends. But Lake Erie was rather wet just the same. And Benjamin wished he had brought his goloshes to keep his feet dry.

As our weary bear crawled out of the water, he was greeted by a group of cheering football fans. They took Benjamin to the famous Cleveland Clinic for a check-up to make sure all his stuffing was still in the right place. One of the largest private medical centers in the country, the Cleveland Clinic probably performs more heart surgery than any other hospital in the country. But Benjamin wasn't really very concerned about his heart:...because he didn't have a heart.

Later Benjamin was whisked to City Hall, a beautiful, big building with tall pillars. There, a man called the mayor, who is in charge of the city, patted him on the head and said what a good bear he was. Then the mayor presented Benjamin with an important-looking piece of paper that said how glad Cleveland was that he played for the Browns and not for the "Bears" or some other team.

Because he was a football hero, Benjamin was invited to visit the Cleveland schools, which are among the best in the country. The children hoisted Benjamin up in the air and cheered, "Horray for Benjamin, the best ball the Browns ever had!" Many of them asked Benjamin for his autograph. But since he couldn't write, he wasn't very good at giving autographs.

Along about this time, Benjamin became tired of being a hero. And besides, he missed Missy. So he headed for the quietest place he could find—the Cleveland Public Library, one of the nation's leading libraries.

There, a very kind-looking lady with tiny glasses, named Mrs. Munchleaf, leaned across her desk and inquired, "May I help you, please?" She told Benjamin that, no, she didn't have any books about little lost girls. But she suggested that he read a book called "Winnie the Pooh". Benjamin decided that a whole book about a stuffed bear sounded silly. Besides, his nose was twitching. So he left.

Moses Cleaveland was the next person Benjamin met as he left the library. Moses Cleaveland stood straight and tall and very, very silent. He even had his name carved in stone at his feet, which seemed like a good idea to Benjamin. He thought everyone should have his name carved at his feet, so you could tell who people were without ever asking.

Moses Cleaveland led a party of settlers out of Connecticut and discovered Cleveland in 1796, 20 years after the Declaration of Independence was signed. It occurred to Benjamin that if Moses Cleaveland could discover the entire city, then he certainly could help find a little lost girl.

But Moses Cleaveland didn't seem to move much. Perhaps that was just as well, for if he moved more, he might wander around and find other cities and call them Cleveland. And Benjamin thought it was nice to have only one Cleveland.

Over at the lovely, tree-lined Public Mall, a generous young man offered Benjamin half a sandwich. He gratefully accepted and sat down on the edge of the fountains to refill his fuzzy, little body. Before long he began to feel stuffed—stuffed bears often feel this way. Benjamin yawned, stretched, leaned back—and fell KER-SPLASH into the fountain.

Fortunately, a mounted policeman the children called "Big Bill" happened by just as Benjamin took his plunge. Big Bill rescued the Browns' beloved, four-legged football from the very wet water and scooped Benjamin up into the saddle with him. Benjamin asked Big Bill if he would help find Missy. "This is a very big city in which to find such a small girl," smiled Bill, "but I'll try to help."

The unlikely twosome rode up Euclid Avenue, Cleveland's main downtown street. As they rode into Playhouse Square, Benjamin suddenly spotted Batman and Robin climbing down the wall of a nearby building—presumably to help find Missy. It would perhaps have been more appropriate had Superman arrived on the scene. For it was Superman who was created here in Cleveland—not on Krypton—by two Glenville High School students back in 1933.

When Batman and Robin did not appear to be making much progress down the wall, Benjamin became impatient and suggested that they not wait for the "dynamic duo" any longer. Big Bill just roared with laughter.

Bill said he would report that Missy was missing. Then he dropped Benjamin off at the Natural History Museum, where Benjamin mentioned he had some distant relatives. Benjamin wandered through the many wonders of the museum, looking for Missy. Along the way, he kept running into animals who used to be real but were now just as stuffed as he was. Then he happened upon the biggest bunch of bones he had ever seen.

The bones were named Haplocanthosaurus. He was a dinosaur. Or rather, he used to be a dinosaur. Benjamin thought he should eat more. And he told him so. Then Benjamin asked if he had seen Missy. But Haplocanthosaurus just stood there looking mean and boney. So Benjamin left.

He waddled down the street past Severance Hall, home of the Cleveland Orchestra—one of the finest orchestras in the world. Benjamin was in Cleveland's unique University Circle area, where the Natural History Museum, Severance Hall, the Garden Center, the Institute of Art, the Institute of Music, the Western Reserve Historical Society, the Art Museum and the Auto-Aviation Museum are all within walking distance of each other.

Benjamin soon found his way to the Art Museum. After looking at lots of pretty paintings, he came upon a room full of creatures from outer space. The creatures were all wearing strange steel suits that looked like they belonged in a movie. They also looked very uncomfortable.

Benjamin overheard a pretty school teacher tell her students that the "creatures" were actually suits of armor worn by knights a long, long time ago. They still seemed to be wearing the armor as far as he could tell. Perhaps these knight or day creatures, or whatever they were, had kidnapped Missy, thought Benjamin. He climbed up an armored horse and was preparing to yell, "Where are you holding Missy captive?" into the mounted knight's helmet, when he slipped.

He slipped off the knight's shoulder, bounced "clank" off his arm, "clink" off his hand, and then slid "wheee" all the way down his long steel leg. He dangled for a moment on the knight's tin toe, and then fell right into a baby carriage that was being wheeled past by a talkative young mother.

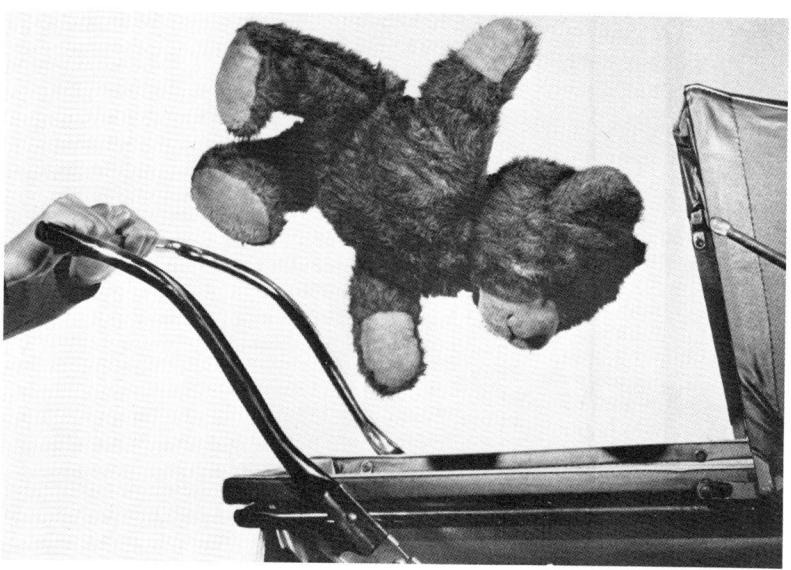

"Oh, what a cutey-wooty little bear," squealed the mother. "Gub, gub," gurgled the baby. "Help!", thought Benjamin. "Baby want to go shopping?", cooed the mother. "Burp," responded the baby. "Oh yuk," thought Benjamin.

Benjamin would have departed rather hastily had it not been for the very firm head-hold the baby had on him. So mother and baby and Benjamin all drove to Randall Park Mall, the largest indoor shopping mall in the United States. There, the baby tired of Benjamin's company and tossed him rather abruptly out of the carriage.

Benjamin was so happy to be free again that he began racing recklessly through the mall. He spilled perfume all over a stern-looking man, who then smelled prettier than his wife for the rest of the day. He knocked over three cages and sent five hamsters scampering around a pet shop. And finally he slid down one of the long bannisters into a startled lady's lap.

The lady turned Benjamin over to a sales clerk in a toy store. And the clerk tied Benjamin to a shelf among a whole zoo full of other stuffed animals. A tear rolled down to the tip of Benjamin's nose and dropped on one of his paws. He was very sad. Now he would never be able to find his dear friend Missy.

Then one day, a tall, smiling man walked into the toy store and bought Benjamin. The tall, smiling man tied a big bow around Benjamin's neck and took him for a ride in his car. The car stopped in front of a familiar-looking house, and the man carried our fuzzy friend in with him.

Inside, he presented Benjamin to a cute little girl who was wearing a pretty dress and a big, wide grin. Who do you think the little girl was?

You're right. She was Benjamin's Missy.

Missy had not been lost after all. She had just gone down the street to play. And the tall, smiling man was Missy's Uncle Max, who brought her a present when he came to dinner—not knowing that the bear he brought was none other than Missy's beloved Benjamin.

Missy said, "Thank you" to her Uncle Max, and "I missed you" to Benjamin. She hugged him harder than he had ever been bear-hugged before. And that made him feel all warm and fuzzy inside.

Benjamin's nose wasn't twitching any more. And he thought to himself, "Cleveland really is a warm, fuzzy place!"